# DINOSAURS IN 30 SECONDS

First published in the UK in 2016 by Ivy Kids.
This edition published in the US in 2017 by

**Ivy Kids**

An imprint of The Quarto Group
The Old Brewery
6 Blundell Street
London N7 9BH
United Kingdom
www.QuartoKnows.com

ISBN: 978-1-78240-529-0

This book was conceived, designed & produced by

**Ivy Kids**

58 West Street, Brighton BN1 2RA, United Kingdom

| | |
|---|---|
| PUBLISHER | Susan Kelly |
| CREATIVE DIRECTOR | Michael Whitehead |
| COMMISSIONING EDITOR | Hazel Songhurst |
| MANAGING EDITOR | Susie Behar |
| PROJECT EDITOR | Robin Pridy |
| ART DIRECTOR | Hanri van Wyk |
| DESIGNER | Emily Portnoi |
| DESIGN ASSISTANT | Emily Hurlock |
| EDITORIAL ASSISTANT | Lucy Menzies |

Printed in China

1 3 5 7 9 10 8 6 4 2

# DINOSAURS
## IN 30 SECONDS

### SEAN CALLERY

ILLUSTRATED BY SAM HUBBARD
CONSULTANT: JONATHAN TENNANT

# Contents

# About this book

## ... in 60 seconds

Why are dinosaurs so fascinating? Is it their incredible size? Some were as long as five buses. Others were as tall as a five-story building. Or perhaps it's their looks—razor-sharp teeth and claws as long as daggers, strange horns, and head crests, and long spikes on their tails and backs. Some dinosaurs even had wings and feathers. They were like real-life dragons or monsters.

This book will take you on a journey back in time, to around 225 million years ago, when dinosaurs ruled Earth. The "Age of Dinosaurs" lasted 160 million years—about 800 times longer than humans have been around. Continents were tearing apart and crunching together, creating mountain ranges, thousands of erupting volcanoes, and even entire seas and oceans.

It was a world of extremes, where it was often "kill or be killed." Only the fiercest or biggest dinosaurs weren't hunted by other dinosaurs. You can explore this amazing world of enormous swampy forests, toxic lagoons, and vast deserts with deadly sandstorms, and find dinosaurs alongside gigantic insects, sea creatures, and flying reptiles.

But how do we know all this existed? Paleontologists, of course! These dinosaur detectives dig up the truth on how these great beasts lived so long ago. Discover how a few bones and teeth found in the ground, or even just a footprint, can reveal what a dinosaur looked like, what it ate, or even how fast it ran.

Yet many dinosaur mysteries remain. What was their skin color? What did they sound like? We don't know for certain. We know they died out quickly, but there are still questions about how and why. Will we ever really know the true stories of these incredible creatures? Get your tools ready as we prepare to dig deeper ...

# Life begins

About 4.6 billion years ago, Earth was a rocky planet with molten lava flowing over its surface. It had no breathable air and no water. After billions of years, water formed and life began to develop. The first living things were bacteria, followed by simple sea creatures. When plants began to grow on land, animals moved from the water onto land, too. The lizardlike creatures that thrived at this time were some of the earliest relatives of Earth's largest land animals—the dinosaurs.

# Life begins
# Glossary

**adapt** To become better suited to the environment.

**amphibian** An animal (such as a frog or toad) that can live both on land and in water.

**ancestor** An animal that was historically related to another animal in the past (a grandmother is the ancestor of her granddaughter).

**archosaur** A group of reptiles that includes dinosaurs and crocodiles.

**armor** A hard, protective covering over the body of an animal.

**arthropod** A group of animals, such as insects, spiders, and prawns, with a segmented body and no backbone.

**bacteria** The simplest and smallest forms of life, too small to see without a microscope.

**climate** The average pattern of weather for a particular area.

**conifer** An ancient tree with cones and needlelike leaves.

**continent** One of Earth's seven major areas of land: Africa, Antarctica, Asia, Australia, Europe, North America, and South America.

**cycad** An ancient palmlike plant.

**descended** Came from an **ancestor** (a daughter is descended from her parents).

**era** A division of time within the geological time scale, within which are periods, such as the Jurassic.

**evolution** The way that all living things developed, over long periods of time, from earlier life forms.

**evolve** To develop gradually.

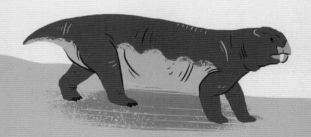

**fossil** Animal or plant remains that have turned into rock.

**genetic changes** Traits that pass on to your **descendants**.

**geology** The study of the origin, history, and structure of Earth.

**gingko** An ancient tree with fan-shaped leaves and yellow flowers.

**horsetail** An ancient plant with a stem, narrow leaves, and cones.

**mammal** An animal that has a backbone, breathes air, and grows hair. The female produces milk to feed its young.

**MYA** The abbreviation for "millions of years ago."

**nautiloid** One of the first groups of sea creatures with an external shell.

**nutrient** The substance in food that is needed to survive and be healthy.

**organism** An individual life form.

**oxygen** A chemical found in the air, which has no color, taste, or smell, and that is needed for life.

**paleontologist** A scientist who studies fossils and the history of life.

**predator** An animal that lives by killing and eating other animals.

**rain forest** A forest that receives a lot of rain and has very tall trees.

**stratum** (plural: strata) A layer of rock, usually one of many.

**tetrapod** An animal with four limbs and a backbone.

**therapsid** A mammal-like reptile from the Permian and Triassic periods.

**time scale** A period of time that it takes for something to happen.

**trilobite** One of the first groups of sea creatures with a hard skeleton.

**vegetation** All the plants or plant life of a place.

# Geological time scale
## ... in 30 seconds

Beneath the ground you're on right now, there are layers upon layers of rock. All of these layers, known as strata, form Earth. These strata reach far down below the ground we walk on—imagine the layers of your favorite cake and you've got the right idea!

When put together, these layers show us all the periods of time, from Earth's beginnings to now—this is the geological time scale. Measured in "millions of years ago" (MYA), this time scale shows what happened on Earth from the continents shifting together and breaking apart again to volcanic eruptions, mass extinctions, and new types of animals and plants.

By inspecting these layers of rock, scientists can even understand what the climate was like. Fossils of plants and animals can also be found in these layers, allowing us to see what kinds of life there was on Earth.

This has helped us discover the extraordinary "Age of Dinosaurs," which lasted for 160 million years (humans have only been around for 200,000 years), when they were the largest, most fearsome creatures on land.

## 3-second sum-up

The geological time scale divides up time from Earth's beginnings to the present day.

## 3-minute mission Do your own dig

**You need:** • Small digging tool • Small paintbrush • Container • Twine • 4 clothespins • 4 sticks

**1** Choose your site and stake out a square with your 4 sticks.

**2** Run the twine around the sticks, fastening the string with a clothespin to each stick.

**3** Start digging! If you find a fossil (a bone, stone, or seedpod), brush it off with your paintbrush, then place it in the container.

# Earth's layers, and what's found in them, show the different time periods from our planet's beginnings to the present day.

| Cenozoic era | Quaternary (2.6 MYA–present) |
| | Neogene (23–2.6 MYA) |
| | Paleogene (66–23 MYA) |

**Mesozoic era**

Cretaceous (145–66 MYA) { Late / Early

Jurassic (201–145 MYA) { Late / Middle / Early

Triassic (252–201 MYA) { Late / Middle / Early

**Paleozoic era**

Permian (299–252 MYA)

Carboniferous (359–299 MYA)

Devonian (419–359 MYA)

Silurian (444–419 MYA)

Ordovician (485–444 MYA)

Cambrian (541–485 MYA)

Pre-Cambrian (4.6 billion years ago to 541 MYA)

# What is evolution?

## ... in 30 seconds

 Evolution takes a long, long time. We are descended from fish, but a fish didn't just wake up one morning, walk onto land, and make a cup of coffee! Human evolution alone has taken five million years, and it's taken more than three billion years to get from the first bacteria to us.

Fish needed air sacs to breathe on land, muscular fins to "walk," and thousands more changes before they could move onto land, let alone develop a thumb and finger to hold a cup.

 But how do these changes happen? Sometimes, a living thing develops a different feature than its parents. Perhaps a baby dinosaur is born with "fuzz" on its body—this is often due to a genetic change. Something in that baby's DNA, a kind of code that tells our bodies how to grow, allowed fuzz to emerge.

In a cold winter, that fuzz may have kept the dinosaur warmer while its brothers and sisters died of cold. That fuzzy dinosaur then had loads of fuzzy babies that all survived the colder winters ... Fast forward a few million years and we have feathered dinosaurs! They had adapted over time to keep warmer by having fuzz and then feathers. The dinosaurs had evolved.

## 3-second sum-up

Animals and plants change slowly over time.

## 3-minute mission Convergent evolution

To survive, most living things need to develop defenses against predators. Even though they look completely different, some plants and animals can have strangely similar features—this is called convergent evolution. Take a guess in this example: "I have grown spikes to defend myself against things that want to eat me. What am I?" See the answers on page 96.

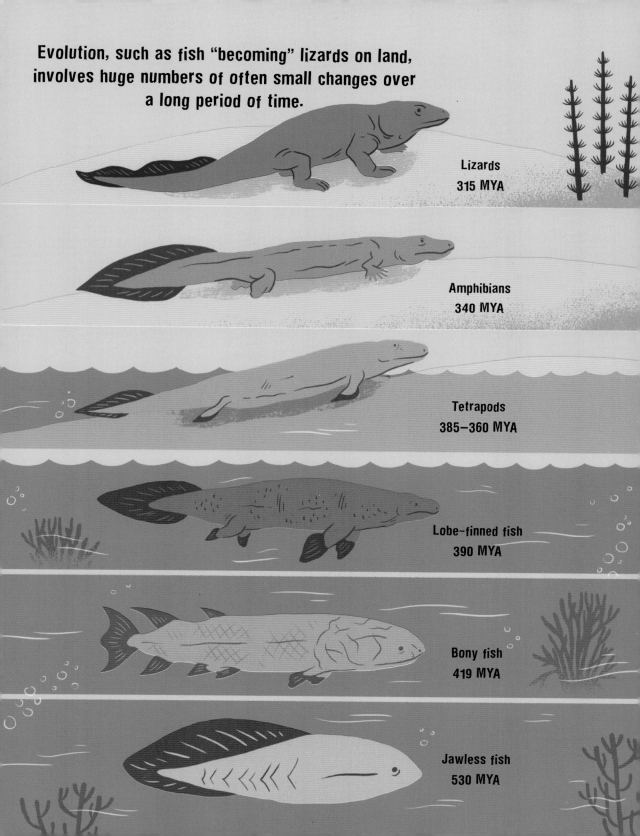

Evolution, such as fish "becoming" lizards on land, involves huge numbers of often small changes over a long period of time.

Lizards
315 MYA

Amphibians
340 MYA

Tetrapods
385–360 MYA

Lobe-finned fish
390 MYA

Bony fish
419 MYA

Jawless fish
530 MYA

# First life

## ... in 30 seconds

About 4.6 billion years ago, Earth was a hot, fiery rock. The air was too toxic for life. But as it cooled, Earth formed two essential things for life: oxygen and water.

The first life forms were bacteria, which grew in shallow seas. Tiny worms and simple creatures, such as starfish and sponges, developed, followed by hard-bodied trilobites and nautiloids. It took billions of years, but by the Devonian period (419 to 359 MYA), Earth's seas and lakes were full of fish, such as sharks and eels—there were even coral reefs. A lot had happened!

Plants, at first just a few inches tall, sprouted up along the water's edge and became plentiful. This is probably what drew arthropods, early ancestors of spiders and insects, to shore. These millipede-like creatures were the first land animals on Earth.

The seas continued to fill up with all kinds of animals, from giant sea scorpions to armored fish. But about 390 MYA, a special kind of fish went ashore. Using its muscular fins to "crawl" onto land, the lobe-finned fish would leave the swampy inland seas for short periods of time. Dinosaurs (and even you and me!) are descended from these first tetrapods, or four-limbed animals.

## 3-second sum-up

Life started underwater and expanded onto land.

## Why did fish venture onto land?

Some scientists believe that fish moved onto land to find new bodies of water as their old water holes dried up. Others think fish adapted to tides that sometimes left them on land. Another idea is that the "limbs" on these fish may have helped them avoid predators or even hunt in shallow water that may have had roots and tree trunks in it.

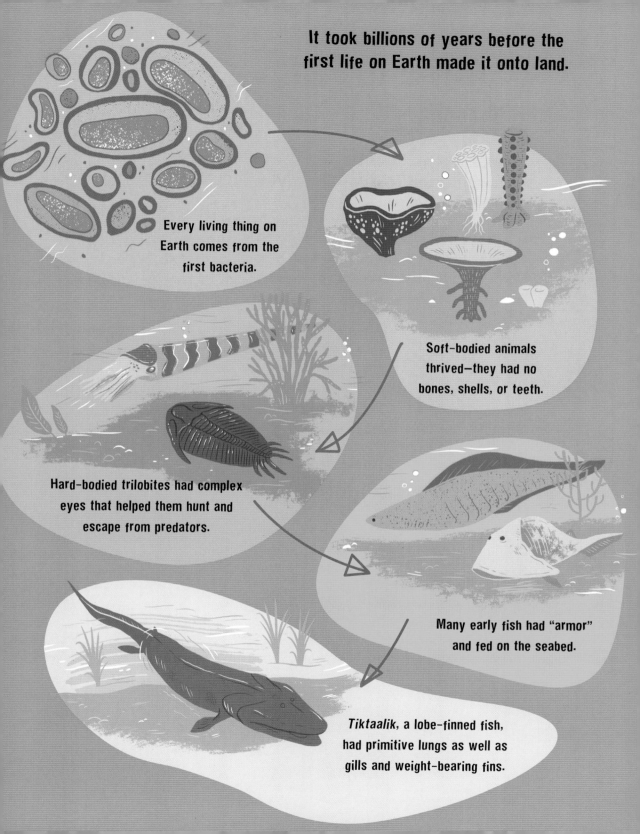

**It took billions of years before the first life on Earth made it onto land.**

Every living thing on Earth comes from the first bacteria.

Soft-bodied animals thrived—they had no bones, shells, or teeth.

Hard-bodied trilobites had complex eyes that helped them hunt and escape from predators.

Many early fish had "armor" and fed on the seabed.

*Tiktaalik*, a lobe-finned fish, had primitive lungs as well as gills and weight-bearing fins.

# The move to land
## ... in 30 seconds

In the Carboniferous Period (359—299 MYA), warm, shallow seas teemed with life, and Earth's continents began moving together to form the supercontinent Pangaea.

**Vast swamps and forests with trees as tall as high-rise buildings were releasing a lot of oxygen into the hot and humid air. Insects thrived in this oxygen-rich environment and grew enormous. There were flying insects as big as sea gulls and millipedes nearly as long as a car.**

The bony fish that crawled onto land about 390 MYA were also adapting. These early tetrapods had long tails, fishlike scales, and wide-splayed limbs. They ate insects and fish. Some became twice as long as a Komodo dragon, today's largest lizard. They were spending more time on land but, like all amphibious creatures, still needed water to survive and hatch their eggs.

Over time, tetrapods developed lungs to breathe air and skin that wouldn't dry out when away from water. Their eggs became hardened, breathable shells that could hatch on land. It was these eggs that allowed them to live entirely on land. These were some of the earliest ancestors of dinosaurs.

## 3-second sum-up

The first amphibious animals evolved to live entirely on land.

## Giant!

*Meganeura* was an enormous dragonfly-like insect, with a wingspan of up to 3.4 ft (1 m). It ate other insects and also small amphibians. Why was it so big? Scientists believe that the gigantic size of some Carboniferous creatures was due to the air, which had three times the amount of oxygen than is present in the air today. Oxygen enables body tissues to grow, so the more oxygen a creature can breathe in, the larger it can grow.

In the Carboniferous period, giant insects and early tetrapods developed on land.

Earth's continents, 360 MYA

*Meganeura* was as large as a sea gull.

Amphibious *Hylonomus* could lay its eggs on land.

Trees grew as tall as the Statue of Liberty in New York and Big Ben in London.

Many animals, such as *Diplocaulus*, still laid eggs in the sea.

*Arthropleura* only ate plants.

*Acanthostega* had fins that were like legs, but it stayed in the sea.

# First reptiles
## ... in 30 seconds

During the late Carboniferous period, the continents began to merge into the supercontinent Pangaea. The climate cooled and became drier. The world's vast rain forests collapsed. "Islands" of tough conifers and cycads took their place, surrounded by large areas of desert. Many amphibians couldn't adapt to these changes and died out.

**Animals that could lay their eggs on land, however, did well in this drier world during the Permian period (299—252 MYA). They evolved into reptiles and developed a harder outer body that wouldn't dry out. Like today's alligators and lizards, they used the Sun's warmth to heat their bodies.**

One particular group of reptiles known as therapsids took center stage. Mammal-like, with legs tucked beneath their bodies, they had two extra holes in their skulls that made their heads lighter and more movable. *Gorgonops* had large fangs to hunt, while *Moschops*, as big as a Siberian tiger, used its strong jaws to chew tough vegetation. Small *Diictodon* sheltered undergound, much like a modern gopher. These new features helped therapsids survive in the harsher Permian world, and they certainly came in handy for several of their later mammal relatives.

## 3-second sum-up

Large, mammal-like reptiles were plentiful in the Permian period.

## False dinosaurs

*Dimetrodon*, with a large sail on its back, is often mistaken for a dinosaur. But it became extinct some 40 million years before the first dinosaurs. Looking like a cross between a large lizard and a dinosaur, it was more closely related to mammals than to modern reptiles. Another set of imposters, archosaurs, looked like crocodiles but walked on two legs. They weren't far off, as they were the early ancestors of dinosaurs and crocodiles, but don't be fooled!

As supercontinent Pangaea began to come together, mammal-like reptiles took over.

There was little or no rain in the center of Pangaea, which became a vast desert.

Pangaea, 299 MYA

Conifers and cycads began to grow during the Permian period.

*Moschops* probably spent a lot of time eating plants to get enough nutrients.

Rabbit-size *Diictodon* lived in burrows, where it sheltered its eggs.

Wolflike *Gorgonops* was a great hunter, helped by two 5-in (12-cm) long fangs.

# Permian period extinction
## ... in 30 seconds

By the Permian period, the planet had come a long way from its lifeless beginnings. Life was plentiful. But about 252 MYA, massive volcanic eruptions blasted out gases and ash that heated, then suddenly cooled Earth.

In the Permian-Triassic Mass Extinction, as it is known, nearly all sea life and 70 percent of land animals died out. They became extinct; entire species were wiped out forever. Pangaea now accounted for almost all of the land on Earth and was surrounded by one ocean, Panathalassa. Desert covered the continent's hot, dry center; summers were baking and winters freezing cold.

Life took millions of years to recover. Survivors, such as the therapsid *Lystrosaurus,* lived near the milder coastal areas, where plants such as ferns, mosses, horsetails, and gingkos provided food.

Crocodile-like archosaurs, which suited hot and dry climates, began to take over. *Euparkeria* was one of the first. It lived in what is now South Africa. Large eyes mean it might have lived in low light or hunted at night, and it may have even spent some time on two legs, using its tail for balance.

## 3-second sum-up

Mass extinction wiped out most life, but new groups of reptiles thrived.

## 3-minute mission Erupting volcano!

Make your own smoking volcano. **Warning!** Adult supervision required, as well as safety goggles and gloves.
**You need:** 2 tbsp baking soda • 1 narrow-necked glass bottle • 4 tbsp vinegar • 1 balloon • **An adult helper**
1 Put the baking soda into the glass bottle.
2 Pour in the vinegar and immediately fit a balloon over the bottle.
3 The vinegar and soda will fizz, releasing bubbles of carbon dioxide that will inflate the balloon.

# Dinosaurs arrive

About 225 MYA, small dinosaurs took their first steps on Earth. There weren't many of them, and they looked nothing like the enormous beasts we think of today. Some became plant-eaters; others hunted and ate meat. Some walked on four legs; others walked on two. By the end of the Triassic period, they had become the largest and most dominant animals on land.

# Dinosaurs arrive
## Glossary

**ancestor** An animal that was historically related to another animal in the past (a grandmother is the ancestor of her granddaughter).

**armor** A hard, protective covering over the body of an animal.

**avian** Something that relates to birds.

**bipedal** An animal that walks on two legs.

**conifer** An ancient tree with cones and needlelike leaves.

**descendant** A living thing that came from an **ancestor** before it (a daughter is a descendant of her parents).

**dromaeosaur** A type of theropod that had long claws and ran fast on two legs.

**extinction** The dying out of an entire species of plant or animal.

**fern** An ancient plant with feathery fronds and spores instead of flowers.

**fossil** The remains of a plant or animal preserved in soil or rock.

**horsetail** An ancient plant with a stem, narrow leaves, and cones.

**Middle Ages** The period of European history between 500—1500 CE.

**MYA** The abbreviation for "millions of years ago."

**omnivorous** An animal that eats plants and animals.

**paleontologist** A scientist who studies fossils and the history of life.

**Pangaea** Earth's supercontinent that existed during the time of dinosaurs.

**prey** An animal that is hunted or killed by another animal.

**pterosaur** A flying reptile from the time of dinosaurs.

**scavenger** An animal that feeds on dead or rotting plants or animals.

**species** A group of animals or plants that are similar and can produce young animals or plants.

**spinosaur** A type of theropod that had a row of "spines" along its backbone.

**vegetation** All the plants or plant life of a place.

**venomous** An animal that injects venom through a bite or sting.

# First dinosaurs

## ... in 30 seconds

After the Permian-Triassic Mass Extinction, it took many more millions of years for plants and animals to recover in the Triassic period. But eventually the coastal areas returned to life. Large trees such as conifers and cycads, as well as plants, such as horsetails and ferns, thrived. Insects and the small ancestors of mammals lived alongside reptiles. This included the close cousins of dinosaurs, winged pterosaurs, which had taken to the air. Fish in the sea began to grow in number and some reptiles even returned to the water.

**The Triassic period is the beginning of a period of time often called the "Age of Dinosaurs," but it didn't happen overnight. It took millions of years before dinosaurs would become the most plentiful and widespread animals on land.**

But what was the first dinosaur? Scientists aren't certain, but they have some good ideas. They know that three types—theropods, sauropodomorphs, and ornithischians—were the first to emerge in a world dominated by other much bigger reptiles. They became successful and, as Pangaea began to break apart at the end of the Triassic, dinosaurs were the main reptiles to survive.

## 3-second sum-up

At first, dinosaurs were only a small part of the Triassic world.

## Alongside the dinosaurs

Dinosaurs may have dominated land in the Triassic period but there was plenty of life elsewhere. Ichythyosaurs were a group of marine reptiles that actually returned to the sea. They looked a lot like fish and dolphins, breathed air, and gave birth to live young. One species, *Shonisaurus*, was up to 50 ft (15 m) long. Pterosaurs, descended from archosaurs, began to take flight. Sometimes confused with dinosaurs, these flying reptiles were small at first. One species was the size of a hummingbird, one the size of a crow.

Theropods, sauropodomorphs, and ornithischians were the first types of dinosaur to emerge.

*Saturnalia*, possibly the first sauropodomorph, lived in what is now southern Brazil.

The first mammals appeared in the Triassic and looked like mice.

*Eoraptor*, a theropod, possibly ate both meat and plants, and it walked on two legs.

*Pisanosaurus*, one of the first ornithischians, didn't arrive until the Late Triassic.

Saturnalia     Eoraptor     Pisanosaurus

# Dinosaur types

## ... in 30 seconds

To better understand the thousands of different types of dinosaurs, scientists have placed them into various groups within the overall dinosaur family.

Saurischians are "lizard-hipped." Their pelvis points down and toward the front, as in lizards. Ornithischians are "bird-hipped"—two of their three hip bones point backward and are close together, as in birds. Horned dinosaurs such as *Triceratops* and the armored *Stegosaurus* and *Ankylosaurus* are ornithischians. This group had beaks and only ate plants—some walked on two legs, some on four.

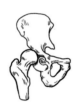

The saurischians are divided into two: the large, plant-eating, four-legged sauropodomorphs such as *Diplodocus* and *Brachiosaurus*, and the meat-eating, two-legged theropods such as dromaeosaurs and spinosaurs. Theropods have several groups, but most are Tetanurae, which have stiff tails and include *Tyrannosaurus rex* and *Velociraptor*.

Another special set of saurischians are the avian dinosaurs, better known as ... birds! Despite the shape of their hips, they are the direct descendants of theropod dinosaurs.

## 3-second sum-up

The many types of dinosaurs have been classed into groups that share features.

## Wrong name!

Despite their name meaning "terrible lizard," dinosaurs are not lizards, partly because of how their legs joined to their bodies. Lizards sprawl, with legs spread out. Dinosaur legs came straight down from their bodies to hold a heavier weight and move faster for longer. Dinosaurs also had extra holes on each side of their skull, possibly to hold their jaw muscles. They laid eggs with hard shells, lived entirely on land, and had thick, leathery skin.

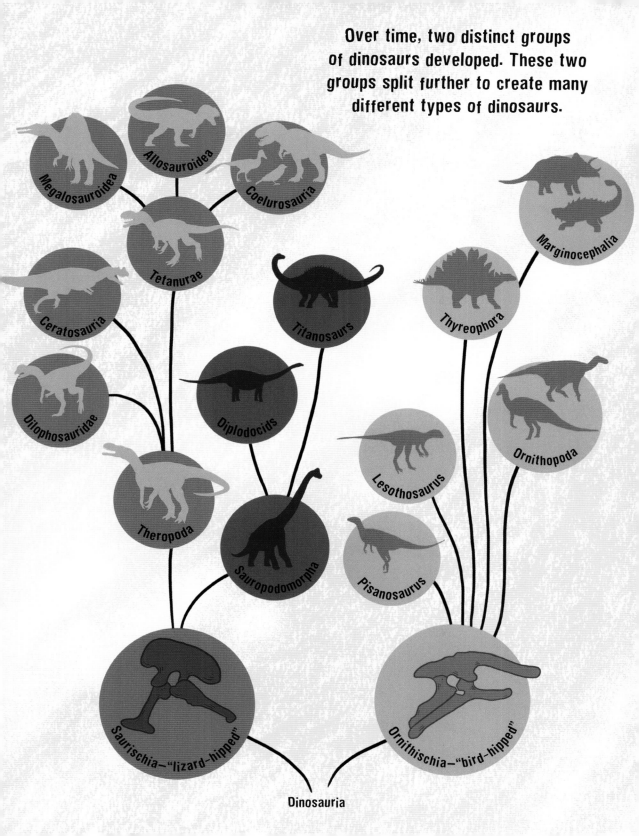

Over time, two distinct groups of dinosaurs developed. These two groups split further to create many different types of dinosaurs.

Megalosauroidea

Allosauroidea

Coelurosauria

Tetanurae

Marginocephalia

Ceratosauria

Titanosaurs

Thyreophora

Dilophosauridae

Diplodocids

Ornithopoda

Theropoda

Lesothosaurus

Sauropodomorpha

Pisanosaurus

Saurischia—"lizard-hipped"

Ornithischia—"bird-hipped"

Dinosauria

# First meat-eaters

## ... in 30 seconds

The earliest dinosaurs included theropods, which appeared in the Late Triassic period (about 230 MYA), but they were not the enormous creatures we think of today. They were often less than 6.5 ft (2 m) long and formed a tiny proportion of Earth's many reptiles.

**Theropods were carnivores—they ate only meat. Strong, clawed fingers, sharp teeth, and the ability to run fast on two legs (they were bipedal) would have allowed them to hunt and scavenge to survive.**

One theropod, *Coelophysis*, was ideal for this. Only 10 ft (3 m) long, it had keen eyesight, sharp hearing, and a large brain. Its lightweight, hollow bones meant it could jump and run fast on its two legs and catch prey. Judging from its different sets of teeth, its earlier relative, *Eoraptor*, may have even been omnivorous, meaning it ate both meat and plants.

The first small theropods passed on these ideal hunting features, which would become even further developed in their much larger and more fearsome descendants, such as *Tyrannosaurus rex*.

## 3-second sum-up

The earliest dinosaurs were small, clawed hunters or scavengers.

## 3-minute mission Hollow bones

Which set of "bones'" can take more weight?
**You need:** • Sheets of paper • 2 paper plates • Wooden blocks or rocks • Adhesive tape
**1** Take four pieces of paper and roll them into separate cylinders, securing them with adhesive tape. Place a paper plate on top of the four cylinders.
**2** Roll up four more pieces of paper so there is little or no hollow section in the cylinder. Place a paper plate on top.
**3** Place a block on each plate, adding one at a time until the cylinders buckle or fall. Which "bones" fell first?

*Coelophysis* probably lived and hunted in family groups.

**Small theropods, such as *Coelophysis*, were some of the earliest meat-eaters.**

Its long tail balanced a flexible neck that could twist and turn to catch animals in its mouth.

Its 80 sharp teeth could easily chop up its dinner.

*Coelophysis* means "hollow form," after the lightweight hollow bones that allowed it to jump and run fast.

It had short forearms and longer legs.

Clawed fingers may have grasped prey.

# First plant-eaters

## ... in 30 seconds

Being smaller suited the first theropods, but being big worked better for the first plant-eating dinosaurs. Known as sauropodomorphs, some of them walked on two legs, some on four. Their larger size protected them from smaller meat-eaters. They also needed big stomachs to digest their big meals. Sauropodomorphs had to eat a lot to survive on the tough vegetation they ate.

**To get food, such as pine needles, sauropodomorphs used their long necks to reach up into the branches. Specially adapted teeth could then strip any vegetation from the cycads and conifers that were their main source of food.**

*Plateosaurus* grew up to 33 ft (10 m) long. More than 50 skeletons have been found in Swabia, Germany, suggesting it may have been common, living in small herds. *Plateosaurus's* nickname is "Swabian Lindworm." Lindworm was a wingless, venomous dragon in tales from the Middle Ages.

When paleontologists first studied *Plateosaurus* fossils, they thought that it walked on four legs. Then they realized that the palms of its "hands" could not face the ground, so it must have walked on two legs. Its thick, heavy tail would have provided much-needed balance.

## 3-second sum-up

Large, plant-eating dinosaurs emerged in the Late Triassic period.

## 3-minute mission Rake it in

In order to strip tree branches and eat the tough vegetation they needed, some sauropodomorphs would "catch" stiff cycad leaves and pine needles in the spaces between their teeth. Try it yourself with a garden rake. Rake the grass (or leaves, if it is fall) and see how it gets caught in the rake's "teeth." If indoors, simply use a comb and run it through long hair. Just don't eat any of it!

**Larger dinosaurs such as *Plateosaurus* were some of the first plant-eaters.**

Its head was small with a long neck and plant-crushing teeth.

*Plateosaurus* mostly walked on two legs, balanced by a big, heavy tail.

Its claws would grab branches and pull them toward its mouth.

These claws may have been used for defense.

Five toes provided *Plateosaurus* with better balance.

# Jurassic period

At the start of the Jurassic period (201 MYA), the supercontinent Pangaea had split into two and continued to drift apart. The planet became warmer and wetter, with shallow seas and thriving plant life. It was a world full of dinosaurs, and they came in all shapes and sizes, from long-necked herbivores six times the weight of an elephant to others with rows of spikes adorning their backs. The herbivores became the perfect prey for fast and large meat-eating theropods.

# Jurassic period
# Glossary

**abundant** When something occurs in large amounts.

**adapt** To become better suited to the environment.

**air chamber** A cavity in a plant or animal that is filled with air.

**air sac** See **air chamber**, above.

**Antarctica** The **continent** that surrounds the South Pole.

**armor** A hard, protective covering over the body of an animal.

**apex** The top of something.

**blood vessel** A channel through which the blood circulates.

**carnivore** An animal that eats other animals.

**climate** The average pattern of weather for a particular area.

**continent** One of Earth's seven major areas of land: Africa, **Antarctica**, Asia, Australia, Europe, North America, and South America.

**crest** A showy growth or tuft of hair on an animal.

**evolve** To develop gradually.

**extinction** The dying out of an entire species of plant or animal.

**fossil** The remains of a plant or animal preserved in earth or rock.

**fungus** (plural: fungi) A plant without flowers (including mushrooms, mold, and yeast) that lives on rotting things.

**gastrolith** A rock held inside an animal to help it grind its food. Found in **sauropods.**

**herbivore** An animal that eats only plants.

**keratin** A tough substance produced by an animal. It is found in hair, nails, horns, and hooves.

**mammal** An animal that has a backbone, breathes air, and grows hair. The female produces milk to feed its young.

**maniraptoran** A group of advanced **theropods** thought to be ancestors of both dinosaurs and birds.

**MYA** The abbreviation for "millions of years ago."

**ornithischian** A member of the group of plant-eating dinosaurs with a birdlike hip.

**Pangaea** Earth's supercontinent that existed during the time of dinosaurs.

**predator** An animal that hunts or kills other animals and eats them.

**preserved** When something is kept from rotting or stays in the same state over a long period of time.

**sauropod** A member of the group of gigantic plant-eating dinosaurs with long necks and small heads.

**scavenged** Fed on dead or rotting plants or animals.

**scutes** A thick, horned, or bony plate on an animal.

**species** A group of animals or plants that are similar and can produce young animals or plants.

**tendon** A strong cord that connects an animal's muscles to its bones.

**theropod** A member of a group of meat-eating dinosaurs that had short arms and ran on two legs.

**vegetation** All the plants or plant life of a place.

# Jurassic world
## ... in 30 seconds

By the Early Jurassic period (201 MYA), Pangaea had split in two. There was Laurasia in the north and a southern landmass called Gondwana, along with thousands of islands, separated by deep oceans or shallow seas. In this warm, moist climate, what were once dry inland areas could now support plants.

Many insects, small mammal-like animals, and reptiles had died out in a mass extinction at the end of the Triassic, making way for dinosaurs to take over on land. These included large numbers of giant sauropods, such as *Vulcanodon* and *Diplodocus,* as well as ornithischians, such as *Stegosaurus.*

These dinosaurs became prey for powerful theropods, such as *Dilophosaurus, Megalosaurus,* and *Allosaurus*. To defend against attacks, many herbivores developed armor, horns, and spikes on their bodies.

As the landmasses continued to break up, dinosaurs couldn't move around as widely. Groups began to evolve on their own. For example, although related, sauropods, such as *Giraffatitan,* were in North Africa, but *Brachiosaurus* remains have been found in North America.

## 3-second sum-up

Dinosaurs evolved separately on Earth's newly emerging landmasses.

## Drifting continents

The landmasses of Gondwana and Laurasia broke up further into the continents that we know today. However, Australia and Antarctica clung together longer, breaking away from each other only 45 million years ago. As Earth's climate cooled, Antarctica started to freeze over, while Australia drifted northward. Even today, the Australian continent moves north at a rate of about 5 inches (2 cm) a year.

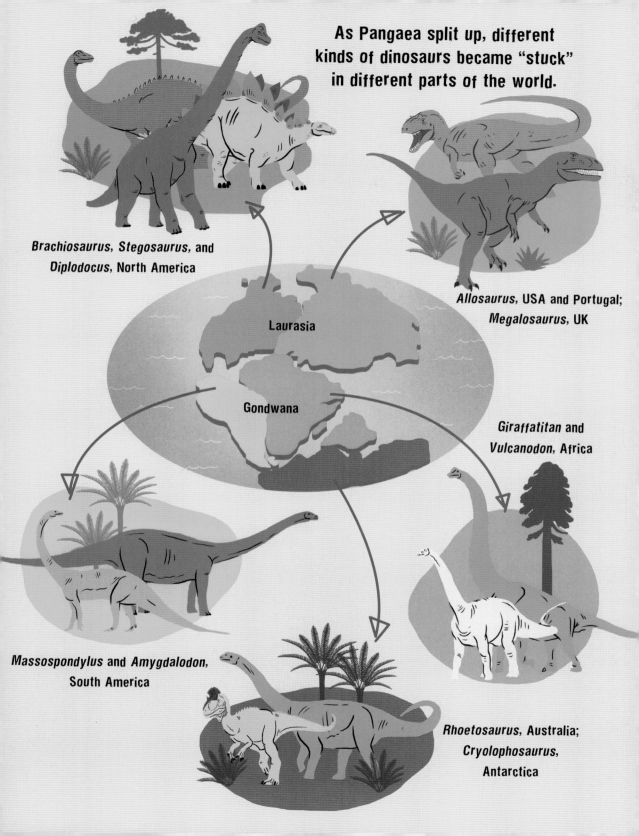

As Pangaea split up, different kinds of dinosaurs became "stuck" in different parts of the world.

*Brachiosaurus*, *Stegosaurus*, and *Diplodocus*, North America

Laurasia

Gondwana

*Allosaurus*, USA and Portugal; *Megalosaurus*, UK

*Giraffatitan* and *Vulcanodon*, Africa

*Massospondylus* and *Amygdalodon*, South America

*Rhoetosaurus*, Australia; *Cryolophosaurus*, Antarctica

# Giant herbivores
## ... in 30 seconds

Long-necked, long-tailed sauropods walked on four sturdy legs and were some of the Jurassic's most abundant dinosaurs. Fully grown, they were about ten times bigger than the largest carnivores at the time.

In North America, *Brachiosaurus* and *Diplodocus* were particularly successful. They would have moved slowly and stayed in groups for protection, possibly even mixing together. *Brachiosaurus* browsed the treetops, munching on tough pine needles, while *Diplodocus* swung its long neck down to reach lower vegetation, raking in ferns with its pencil-like teeth. Neither chewed their food before swallowing it—this gave them time for the important task of eating even more!

*Diplodocus*, at about 108 ft (33 m), was as long as a tennis court. *Brachiosaurus* was slightly smaller but, at about 55 tons, weighed three times as much. This was because *Diplodocus*'s backbone contained air sacs. This made it lighter and more able to hold its neck straight. *Brachiosaurus* also had special features to help it. Large nostrils on top of its head probably brought air into the skull, cooling its brain in the warm climate.

## 3-second sum-up

Sauropods were perfectly adapted to the Jurassic and became common.

## 3-minute mission Stomach aid

Some sauropods swallowed small stones called gastroliths to help digest their tough, leafy food. See how it works.

**You need:** A few small, round pebbles • Plastic container with a lid • Water • 2 lettuce leaves

1 Put the pebbles into the container.
2 Add water and the lettuce leaves, and shut the lid tightly.
3 Shake for a couple of minutes to imitate the movement inside the animal's stomach as it walked.
4 Open the container to see how the leaves are broken up.

Large plant-eaters, such as *Brachiosaurus* and *Diplodocus*, flourished in the Jurassic.

Sauropods had tiny brains for their size—about the size of a human fist.

With its extended neck and unusually long front legs, *Brachiosaurus* could reach the tops of trees for food.

*Diplodocus* only had front teeth, which it used to drag leaves off plants lower down.

*Diplodocus* had an extremely flexible tail that was twice as long as its body.

With their huge stomachs, sauropods could not walk on two legs without falling over.

Brachiosaurus

Diplodocus

# Swift carnivores

## ... in 30 seconds

Large herds of plant-eating sauropods became a main source of food for theropods. Jurassic carnivores evolved special features to catch and eat these animals—stiff tails, for example, improved balance, while strong legs and slim bodies made them powerful, fast runners.

Some of the first dinosaurs known to feast on the larger sauropods included *Cryolophosaurus* and *Monolophosaurus*. They were up to 26 ft (8 m) long, about the length of two or three tigers. They also had head crests, which may have been for display or for making sounds to warn or attract other members of their species.

*Cryolophosaurus* had a crest that ran across the width of its skull. It became known as "Elvisaurus," after the singer Elvis Presley who styled his hair in a quiff. The *Monolophosaurus*'s crest ran down its snout. It was attached to air chambers that may have made its call louder.

These "display" crests show that the dinosaurs may have been social, possibly even traveling in groups. In fact, many fossil skeletons of the crested *Dilophosaurus* (a dinosaur featured, somewhat incorrectly, in the novel and 1993 movie *Jurassic Park*) have been found together.

## 3-second sum-up

Fast and powerful theropods began to prey on the numerous sauropods.

## 3-minute mission What big teeth you have ...

Dinosaur teeth tell us what they ate: sharp for meat, blunt for plants. Use a mirror to look at the types of teeth in your mouth: incisors, canine teeth, and molars. Bite into a carrot with different teeth and investigate what each type of tooth does best. Incisors cut well, canines hold and rip, and molars grind and mash.

**Crested theropods, such as *Cryolophosaurus* were among the first to hunt plant-eating dinosaurs.**

Crests may have been useful for identification and attracting a mate.

*Cryolophosaurus*'s tail was stiffened with strong tendons.

Strong thigh muscles made *Cryolophosaurus* a good sprinter.

Supersharp teeth could slice through thick skin and flesh.

Each hand ended in four fingers.

# Giant predators

## ... in 30 seconds

Meat-eaters got bigger and faster further into the Jurassic period. Some hunted, some scavenged, but all were a threat to almost anything living they met. They were speedy and armed with vicious claws that stabbed and slashed, causing heavy bleeding in their victims.

Apart from their teeth, these dinosaurs' key weapons were claws, which were often daggerlike curved blades. They were made of hard bone and covered in a layer of keratin—the same material as your fingernails and toenails. Many of these carnivores, such as *Yangchuanosaurus*, also evolved a good sense of smell, which improved their hunting skills.

At about 28 ft (8.5 m) long, *Allosaurus* was the largest predator of the Late Jurassic in North America. It probably attacked smaller prey such as *Stegosaurus* alone, but it may have joined a pack to hunt large sauropods, such as *Diplodocus*. *Allosaurus* was a real battler. Many fossil skeletons show injuries suffered as victims fought back.

## 3-second sum-up

Jurassic meat-eaters were truly terrifying predators.

## The food chain

Living things need food to survive, whether it's other animals, other plants, or even dirt! The "chain" is the link to what eats what. In Jurassic times, plants used sunlight to make food, an insect ate the plant, a small dinosaur caught the insect, then a larger dinosaur ate the smaller dinosaur. This dinosaur was at the top of the food chain, because there wasn't anything that could hunt it. After it died, however, insects, small animals, or fungi would have fed on its carcass. After rotting and being partially eaten, the carcass would become... dirt! The entire cycle could start all over again.

**Meat-eaters, such as *Allosaurus*, preyed on large plant-eaters.**

*Allosaurus* had two crests above its eyes that could have provided shade from the Sun.

It had widely spaced eyes almost on the side of its head. This means its vision may not have been that good.

Powerful jaws held about 70 sharp teeth.

Three sharp, hooked claws gripped victims until it could sink its teeth into the throat.

*Allosaurus* had three main toes and a fourth one on the inner side of each foot.

# Dinosaur defenses
## ... in 30 seconds

In the Jurassic period, ornithischian dinosaurs developed new ways to fight off or run from predators. Some had spiky tails and bony plates (called scutes) on their bodies, while smaller dinosaurs became speedy, darting out to eat plants the larger herbivores couldn't reach.

**Scutellosaurus was one of the first dinosaurs to have this kind of armor. It had 300 bony plates covering its back and tail. If caught by a predator, it would crouch down and its plates could fend off body blows, teeth, or claws.**

The much smaller *Othnielia* did not have armor, but its special weapon was that it could run very fast, with a stiff tail that helped it balance. It could also eat plants close to the ground, which gigantic sauropods, such as *Brachiosaurus,* couldn't reach.

By the Late Jurassic period, larger armored dinosaurs, such as *Stegosaurus,* were common. At 30 ft (9 m) long, and weighing about 7.5 tons, herds slowly wandered through woodlands and plains in search of fresh leaves and shoots. Their size, the double row of 17 plates on their back, and a lethal, spiked tail kept many predators away.

## 3-second sum-up

Ornithischians ran fast or developed armor and spikes to protect themselves from predators.

## Should we warm your plates?

Many scientists believe that the bony plates on the backs of stegosaurs, such as *Stegosaurus*, aside from scaring off predators, may have also helped control their body temperature. Skin covering the plates would have carried blood vessels, and blood flowing through them could be warmed by the Sun or cooled in a breeze. These plates, which might have been brightly colored or patterned, may have also helped them find mates.

# Ornithischians, such as *Stegosaurus*, found several ways to ward off predators.

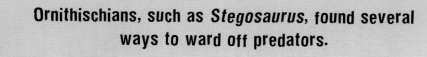

*Stegosaurus's* thin plates may have been used to control its temperature, as well as in defense.

Traveling in herds may have offered extra protection from predators.

**Stegosaurus**

Four spikes on its heavy tail could swing into attackers like a club.

Its brain was the size of a walnut!

Like all ornithischians, it had a beak and cheek pouches adapted to chewing and eating plants.

Lightweight legs and long shins and toes made *Othnielia* fast.

**Othnielia**

Stegosaurus

Othnielia

# Feathers and teeth

## ... in 30 seconds

In the Middle to Late Jurassic, several theropod dinosaurs began to develop in a surprising new way. Fossils found from this time show not only that some of them had feathers on different parts of their bodies, but also that they were starting to use their limbs as wings to glide in the air.

*Archaeopteryx* was one of the first of these, part of the maniraptoran group of theropods. About the size of a raven, it had dinosaur traits, such as teeth in its jaws, claws on its hands and feet, and a long, bony tail. But it also had feathers (although these were too primitive to fly) and limbs that resembled wings. It may have climbed, then launched itself from trees, gliding down in search of flying insects. This dinosaur's fossils have been important not only to the debate about birds' origins but also to questions on how all species evolved on Earth.

Other maniraptorans had feathers but did not leave the ground. *Anchiornis*, about the size of a chicken, is one of the oldest maniraptors found so far. It probably mostly ran on its long legs. Well-preserved fossils show it may have had black-and-white wings and a reddish-colored head. Its feathers may have been used to keep warm or to signal to other members of its species.

## 3-second sum-up

Some small theropods developed birdlike features, such as feathers and wings.

## 3-minute mission Take flight!

Dinosaurs, such as *Archaeopteryxm*, probably stretched out their feathered wings like a glider. Crumple up a piece of paper and drop it. Now hold a sheet of paper high and drop it. See how much slower it falls because more air resists it. The paper sheet is gliding.

Theropods, such as *Archaeopteryx*, developed feathers and wings yet kept many dinosaur features.

*Archaeopteryx* means "ancient wing."

It is thought to have glided down from trees to eat insects.

Early feathers would not have been advanced enough for flying.

# Cretaceous period

This "golden age of dinosaurs" included ferocious meat-eaters, such as *Velociraptor* and *Tyrannosaurus rex,* as well as plant-eating, duck-billed and crested dinosaurs that raised their young and lived in groups. Sauropod dinosaurs grew even larger, mammal numbers increased, and snakes, flowering plants, and bees emerged for the first time. Sea life flourished. But deep underground, there were rumblings. Also, far out in space, something was hurtling toward Earth ...

# Cretaceous period
# Glossary

**ancestor** An animal that was historically related to another animal in the past (for example, a grandmother is the ancestor of her granddaughter).

**aquatic** Living completely or almost completely in the water.

**armor** A hard, protective covering over the body of an animal.

**asteroid** One of thousands of rocky objects in space that moves around the Sun in our solar system.

**bipedal** An animal that walks on two legs.

**brood** To sit on eggs to hatch them.

**conifer** An ancient tree with cones and needlelike leaves.

**continent** One of Earth's seven major areas of land: Africa, Antarctica, Asia, Australia, Europe, North America, and South America.

**debris** The pieces left when something is destroyed.

**descendant** A living thing that came from an **ancestor** before it (a daughter is a descendant of her parents).

**extinction** The dying out of an entire species of plant or animal.

**fossil** The remains of a plant or animal preserved in earth or rock.

**herbivore** An animal that eats only plants.

**hurricane** A violent storm with high winds.

**Ice Age** A period of extreme cold where ice and snow cover most of Earth.

**lava** The hot molten rock from a volcano or a crack in Earth.

**mammal** An animal that has a backbone, breathes air, and grows hair. Females produce milk for their young.

**mammoth** A group of animals that lived during the last great Ice Age. They had long tusks and looked like a large elephant with "woolly" fur.

**megatsunami** An extremely high sea wave caused by earthquakes or volcanic eruptions.

**mimic** To copy something.

**nonavian** Not like birds.

**nuclear bomb** An explosive device that creates huge amounts of energy.

**ornithischian** A member of the group of plant-eating dinosaurs with a birdlike pelvis.

**Pangaea** Earth's supercontinent that existed during the time of dinosaurs.

**plain** A large area of flat land with few trees.

**predator** An animal that hunts or kills other animals and eats them.

**prey** An animal that is hunted or killed by another animal.

**pterosaur** A flying reptile from the time of dinosaurs.

**regulate** To control or maintain something, like temperature or speed.

**retractable** Able to be pulled back inside something larger and pushed out again, like a claw in a digit.

**sauropod** A member of the group of gigantic plant-eating dinosaurs with long necks and small heads.

**scavenger** An animal that feeds on dead or rotting plants or animals.

**species** A group of animals or plants that are similar and can produce young animals or plants.

**talon** A sharp claw, usually on a bird.

**theropod** A member of a group of meat-eating dinosaurs that had short arms and ran on two legs.

**vegetation** All the plants or plant life of a place.

**wildfire** A fire that spreads quickly over a wide area.

# Cretaceous world
## ... in 30 seconds

Pangaea continued to split apart in the Cretaceous period, with new oceans opening up and continents, such as South America and Africa, becoming much as they are now. A warm, wet climate meant there were no polar ice caps, and sea levels were much higher than in modern times. Large parts of today's dry land were underwater, including the American Midwest and southern England.

As the continents drifted apart, different plants and animals were developed on each one. There were more pterosaurs and sea creatures, and on land there were new types of mammals as well as social insects, such as ants and bees. Flowering plants, including broad-leaved trees, began to outnumber ferns, and conifers shifted to higher lands.

These more nutritious plants allowed large herbivores, such as *Triceratops* and *Argentinosaurus,* to thrive, along with many smaller species that ate the ground plants out of their reach. More herbivores also meant more food for fearsome theropods, such as *Velociraptor* and *Tyrannosaurus rex*. These meat-eaters evolved into advanced hunters and scavengers, developing razor-sharp teeth with powerful jaws, retractable claws, and strong, fast legs.

## 3-second sum-up

The Cretaceous period saw a wider variety of dinosaurs as well as new plants and animals.

## A tough job, but ...

Imagine a world without flowers, fruit, or vegetables. That is the world we would live in if there were no bees. Unlike conifers, angiosperms (flowering plants) need something other than wind to spread their seeds. Enter the bee, which evolved to use the plants' pollen for food. Flying from flower to flower, it managed to eat dinner while seeding almost the entire Earth in angiosperms during the Cretaceous period.

Life continued to evolve and become abundant in the Cretaceous period.

Pterosaurs of all kinds ruled the skies.

Insects, such as bees and ants, developed.

Flowering plants and broad-leaved trees provided more food.

Sea creatures, such as mosasaurs, grew enormous.

Feathered dinosaurs evolved into many different species.

Small mammals began to emerge.

# Fighting off the meat-eaters
## ... in 30 seconds

By the Cretaceous period, plant-eaters took on all kinds of shapes and sizes. They ranged from fast, small, dog-size dinosaurs to large armored animals with horns, tusks, and thickened skulls.

**Some walked on two legs, some on four, but they all shared the same problem: predators. To avoid being eaten, ornithischian dinosaurs became particularly good at defending themselves. One group, the ankylosaurs, developed extensive body armor and spiked tails to fend off any hunters.**

Ankylosaurs, such as *Ankylosaurus* and *Euoplocephalus*, had flat plates of bone set into the leathery skin on their neck, back, sides, and tail, which formed a shield to protect all but the underbelly. Their heads were completely encased in armor, too, like a helmet. As slow-moving plant-eaters, they needed it. Instead of running away, they could stand their ground and let their armor protect them from teeth and claws.

Sauropods, still around in the Cretaceous, found another interesting way to combat predators. They became too enormous to be killed and eaten! Some, known as titanosauroids, could reach up to 131 ft (40 m) long, more than twice as long as any meat-eating dinosaur that had ever existed.

## 3-second sum-up

Plant-eating dinosaurs increased in number and developed better defenses.

## Mysterious passages

Ankylosaurids had unusual skulls with a network of air passages running through them, kind of like a roller-coaster track. This flow of air may have stopped the brain from overheating inside the thick bone covering. It could have also improved their sense of smell and even helped them to make sounds. By calling out, they could have attracted a mate or even warned other members of their species if there was danger.

Ornithischians
developed impressive
defenses to fend off
predators.

*Euoplocephalus's* armor
had spikes 6 in
(15 cm) long.

Its tailclub
could crush
dinosaur bones.

**Euoplocephalus**

It even had
armored eyelids.

The best way
to fight an ankylosaur was to flip it
over onto its unarmored belly.

**Argentinosaurus**

*Argentinosaurus*
was as heavy as 14
African elephants!

Argentinosaurus

Euoplocephalus

# Horns and frills

## ... in 30 seconds

Not all dinosaur armor was strictly for defense. Another group of plant-eating dinosaurs known as ceratopsians had intimidating horns and neck "frills" around their heads. But looks can be deceiving— although made of solid bone, many of the frills would not have withstood an attack by a large, meat-eating dinosaur.

**Scientists now think that the horns were probably used to fight with other members of their species, like deer use antlers today. The neck frills may have acted like radiators, releasing heat from the body, or they could have been used to attract mates and scare off rivals—the frill could have even changed color to show mood or as a warning. Each species had its own unique "head armor," possibly to help members identify each other.**

Whatever their use, the frills and horns would have been quite a sight. *Styracosaurus* had a large neck frill with four to six long horns, a smaller horn on each of its cheeks, and a single 2-ft (60-cm) long horn on its nose. Elephant-sized *Triceratops* had a neck frill and three large horns, and *Chasmosaurus* had a huge triangular frill with holes in it, like an enormous sail on the back of its head.

## 3-second sum-up

Ceratopsians developed amazing head "armor" for defense and display.

## Eat up!

Ceratopsians also stood out for their beaks, cheek pouches, and the rows of grinding teeth set back in their jaws. The beak helped them dig out, clip, and cut the tough vegetation they ate to survive. Cheek pouches could hold large amounts of food while special teeth ground up the plant matter at the back of their jaws. There weren't many nutrients in these plants and, because it was so hard to process, they probably had to eat constantly to survive.

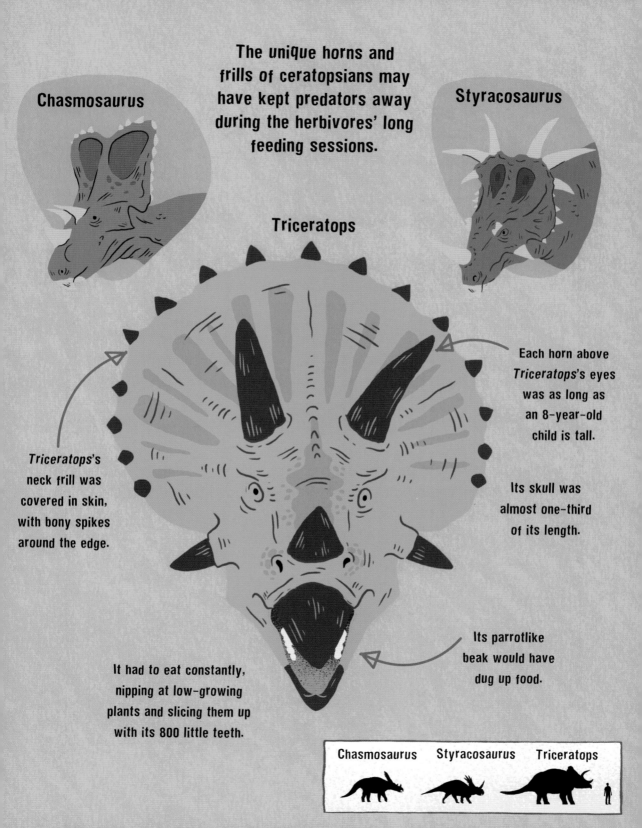

The unique horns and frills of ceratopsians may have kept predators away during the herbivores' long feeding sessions.

**Chasmosaurus**

**Styracosaurus**

**Triceratops**

*Triceratops*'s neck frill was covered in skin, with bony spikes around the edge.

Each horn above *Triceratops*'s eyes was as long as an 8-year-old child is tall.

Its skull was almost one-third of its length.

Its parrotlike beak would have dug up food.

It had to eat constantly, nipping at low-growing plants and slicing them up with its 800 little teeth.

Chasmosaurus    Styracosaurus    Triceratops

# Gigantic predators
## ... in 30 seconds

With so many armored and enormous dinosaurs around, their predators became even more fierce. Of these, the tyrannosaurids are the most well known. These mean flesh-eating machines had massive skulls, balanced by a heavy tail. Their powerful jaws could crunch through bone.

**Many were just a few feet long, but *Tyrannosaurus rex*, at 39 ft (12 m) long and 20 ft (6 m) high, was one of the biggest and most terrifying. It preyed on plant-eaters, such as *Triceratops* and *Anatosaurus*.**

*T. rex* weighed up to 10.5 tons and could run at up to 20 miles per hour. A large brain (possibly larger than a human's), a good sense of smell, and sharp eyesight would have helped it to hunt for prey and find leftover carcasses. It could not chew, so it swallowed whole lumps of meat ripped from its victims.

*T. rex* was big, but *Giganotosaurus*, a carcharodontosaur, was about 6.5 ft (2 m) longer and roamed Earth 30 million years earlier. It had longer arms and weighed 8¼—15½ tons—which is how much food it needed each year to survive. *Giganotosaurus* may have lived and hunted in small groups.

## 3-second sum-up

In the Cretaceous, larger tyrannosaurids and carcharodontosaurs became expert killing machines.

## Seconds, sir?

Big size meant big meals: *T. rex* and *Giganotosaurus* would have needed to eat about 265 human-size victims a year to survive. *T. rex* may have swallowed smaller dinosaurs in one bite. Like *Giganotosaurus*, it would have also hunted larger plant-eating dinosaurs. *T. rex* was also a scavenger, meaning it ate rotting animals. With this much appetite, one wasn't picky!

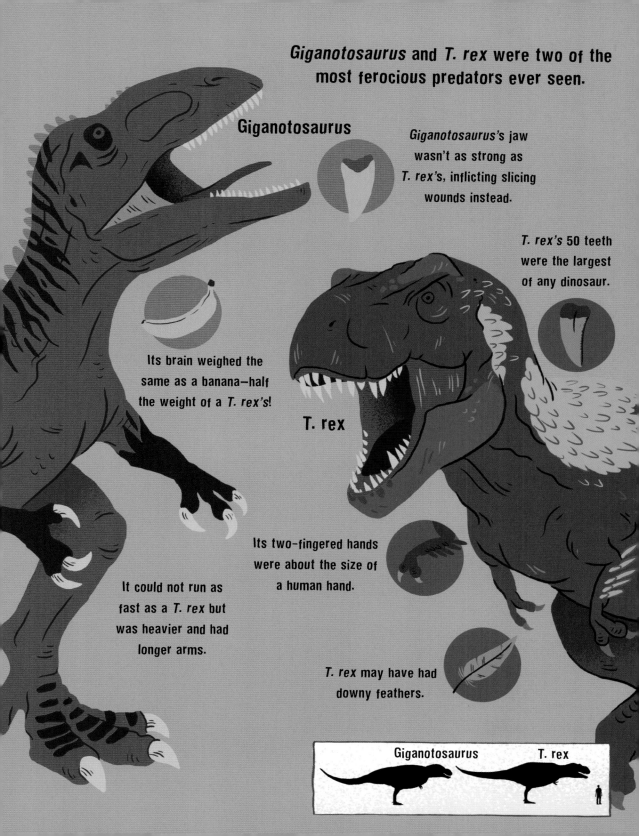

**_Giganotosaurus_ and _T. rex_ were two of the most ferocious predators ever seen.**

**Giganotosaurus**

_Giganotosaurus's_ jaw wasn't as strong as _T. rex's,_ inflicting slicing wounds instead.

_T. rex's_ 50 teeth were the largest of any dinosaur.

Its brain weighed the same as a banana—half the weight of a _T. rex's!_

**T. rex**

Its two-fingered hands were about the size of a human hand.

It could not run as fast as a _T. rex_ but was heavier and had longer arms.

_T. rex_ may have had downy feathers.

Giganotosaurus          T. rex

# Sail-backed spinosaurs
## ... in 30 seconds

In the Cretaceous, the water was teeming with life. It made sense for larger dinosaurs to start catching fish for their supper. The spinosaurids, with their long snouts and jagged teeth that were much like modern crocodiles, were very good at this. Some, such as *Spinosaurus*, may have even swallowed their prey whole while swimming!

*Spinosaurus* could have been up to 56 ft (17 m) long and up to 22 tons in weight, which makes it the biggest-known meat-eating dinosaur. It walked on two legs and had a "sail" on its back. This sail was made from spines covered in thin skin running all the way down its backbone.

The sail may have changed color to attract a mate or helped to regulate the dinosaur's temperature. Blood pumped through the sail could be warmed by the Sun or cooled by a breeze.

*Spinosaurus* was probably semiaquatic, spending plenty of time in the water. It may have even used its sail to change direction as it swam. It ate mostly fish, but it also would have roamed on land to hunt and scavenge other prey, making it one of the Cretaceous period's most fearsome predators.

## 3-second sum-up

The unique-looking Spinosaurus may have been the largest predator to ever walk on Earth.

## 3-minute mission Bigger or smaller?

Here are some of the heaviest animals on the planet today. Do you know if they are heavier or lighter than the *Spinosaurus*? The answers are on page 96.

**African elephant**
**Blue whale**
**Brown bear**
**Saltwater crocodile**

Gigantic *Spinosaurus* had a distinctive enormous sail and crocodile-like snout.

Its large sail may have changed color when blood was pumped through it, like when humans blush!

A *Spinosaurus's* sail may have also held fatty deposits, like a camel.

It may have used its sail to help it swim!

The snout was long and narrow, with straight, cone-shape teeth.

Three long, curved claws could snatch fish or tear into the flesh of a dead body.

# Dromaeosaurs
## ... in 30 seconds

What was the most terrifying dinosaur to ever walk Earth? Most would say a *Tyrannosaurus rex*. But to a dinosaur in Cretaceous times, it was probably a dromaeosaur, sometimes known as a raptor.

**At first glance, these meat-eating theropods may not have seemed that frightening. They were probably covered in feathers and most were small. The biggest, *Utahraptor*, was not much taller than a human, and the smaller ones were about the size of chickens.**

But look closer and it's clear they were effective killers. Fast and bipedal, they probably hunted in packs. A large, curved claw on each second toe may have been used to climb trees. Once caught, an animal wouldn't last long. The dromaeosaur's long, stiff tail would have given balance while it grasped and slashed its prey with three sharp talons on each hand. Long, powerful jaws and sharp teeth would have quickly devoured whatever it caught.

Dromaeosaurs had a big brain for their size and were some of the smartest dinosaurs. Despite this, they still wouldn't have been as smart as your pet cat!

## 3-second sum-up

In the Cretaceous period, raptors were efficient and terrifying killing machines.

## Endo or ecto?

Temperature is a difficult dinosaur topic. We used to believe that all dinosaurs absorbed heat from outside their bodies, from the Sun. This meant they were ectothermic, like modern reptiles. Mammals generate their own heat to maintain body temperature—they are endothermic. Some scientists now believe certain dinosaurs were endothermic, or that they may have had an "in-between," or "mesothermic," way of heating and cooling themselves. Other scientists think this is nonsense! What do you think?

The *Velociraptor's* large eyes may have helped with nighttime hunting.

Dromaeosaurs, such as *Velociraptor*, were perfectly designed for killing prey.

Most dromaeosaurs probably hunted in packs.

Feathers could have been for warmth, or the colors could have signaled to other members of its own species.

The longest toe claw was raised up when walking or running.

All dromaeosaurs have three claws on each hand, with palms facing inward, to grasp prey.

# Birdlike dinosaurs
## ... in 30 seconds

In the Cretaceous period, many theropods developed birdlike features. Ornithomimids, or "ostrich mimics," had a long neck with a small head and a beak without teeth. Fossils have found evidence of feathers, and skin impressions show bare skin instead of scales on parts of their legs. Their long legs meant they were very fast—an *Ornithomimus*, for example, could run as fast as 45 mph (70 kph).

Troodontids, such as *Troodon*, also had long, birdlike legs and probably had feathers. But like raptors, they had a long claw on each foot to slash their prey. With their large brains, they may have been the smartest dinosaurs ever to exist.

Many theropods also acted more like birds. For example, feathered oviraptorids, with beaks more like a parrot's, brooded on their eggs and ate both plants and animals.

Other dinosaurs stir up debate. Scientists disagree on whether pointy-beaked alvarezsaurids, with long legs and birdlike hands, dug up termites for food. And while *Therizinosaurus* had claws 3 ft (1 m) long, it probably used them like giant scythes to gather plant food, rather than to attack other dinosaurs.

## 3-second sum-up

There were several kinds of birdlike dinosaurs in the Late Cretaceous period. Some may yet be classed as birds.

## Simply birds?

Birdlike dinosaurs are part of a large group of meat-eating dinosaurs known as Coelurosauria. This group contains all the feathered dinosaurs and tyrannosaurids, including the enormous *T. rex*. All maniraptorans, such as therizinosauroids, dromaeosaurs, troodontids, oviraptoids, and alvarezsaurids, are in this group, including actual birds.

# Duck-billed dinosaurs
## ... in 30 seconds

Dinosaur bodies changed a lot over millions of years, but that wasn't all that helped them survive. Social behavior was just as important. In fact, this helped hadrosaurs, or duck-billed dinosaurs, become the most common plant-eaters in the Late Cretaceous period.

They travelled in herds, which may have prevented a predator attack. It is likely that *Maiasaura* raised their young, giving them a better chance to survive than if they'd been left to hatch on their own. Other hadrosaurs had extraordinary head crests, probably brightly colored and, besides giving them a keen sense of smell thanks to connected nasal passages, these may have had a social use. *Corythosaurus* and *Parasaurolophus* could have used their crests to make trombonelike "calls" over long distances. The calls may have been used to help them find a mate or to warn others of danger.

Hadrosaurs were also very good at eating plants. Their duck bills, or snouts, scooped up low-lying vegetation. They then used a complex set of grinding teeth to chew. This meant they could digest their food more efficiently, unlike sauropods that swallowed plants whole!

## 3-second sum-up

Socially advanced duck-billed hadrosaurs dominated the Late Cretaceous period.

## 3-minute mission Call like a hadrosaur

Each hadrosaur species may have had a unique call, thanks to hollow tubes connecting its crest to its nostrils. See if you, too, can make your own sounds.
**You need:** 1 length of plastic tube • Scissors • **An adult helper**
1 Get an adult to help you cut short and long pieces of plastic tube.
2 For each different length of tube, hold your thumb or finger tightly against one opening, and blow in at the other end to make a sound. How is each sound different?

Duck-billed dinosaurs, such as *Maiasaura*, looked after their young and lived together.

Hadrosaurs may have lived in large herds.

*Maiasaura* had a flat-topped skull, unlike most hadrosaurs, which had crests.

The name *"Maiasaura"* means "good mother lizard." Fossilized nests have been found with crushed eggshells.

Its eggs were about the size of a basketball.

# Dinosaur extinction
## ... in 30 seconds

Dinosaurs roamed the planet for 160 million years,
but died out in just a few months. How did this happen?

**Many scientists believe it was the combination of a gigantic asteroid
hitting Earth and a series of massive volcanic eruptions that choked the
planet. At the end of the Cretaceous period, the shifting continents were
setting off endless volcanic eruptions. Toxic dust and fumes that stank
of rotten eggs would have filled the air. For about 30,000 years, lava
from erupting volcanoes covered half of India.**

Of course, the asteroid didn't help! It was 6 miles (10 kilometres) wide
when it smashed into Mexico and it was like thousands of nuclear bombs
going off at once, blasting millions of tons of dust, soil, and rock into
the air and causing hurricanes, wildfires, and "megatsunamis."

Dust would have blocked out the Sun for months—plants died and plant-eating
dinosaurs perished. The meat-eaters starved, as did three-quarters of life on
Earth. However, some types of animals lived. Most animals survived underwater
or underground in burrows. Many of these were the ancestors of modern mammals.

## 3-second sum-up

Catastrophic
events at the end
of the Cretaceous
period led to the
extinction of all
nonavian
dinosaurs.

## 3-minute mission Create a crater!

When an asteroid hit the Gulf of Mexico 66 million years ago, its
impact left a massive crater, or hole, in Earth. Make your own!
**You need:** Newspaper • Powder such as powder paint or flour
• Balls of different sizes and weights, such as a marble, a lump
of clay, and an apple
**1** Outdoors, cover the ground with newspaper and then the powder.
**2** Drop the different balls from various heights and watch how each
impact forms a different-sized crater and sends out debris.

Many scientists believe that volcanic eruptions and a massive asteroid hitting Earth led to the end of the Age of Dinosaurs.

Gas and smoke from volcanoes would have already killed off many plants and animals.

Without sunlight, plants and then animals would have died.

The asteroid's impact would have triggered earthquakes, volcanic eruptions, and "megatsunamis."

An asteroid that hits Earth is called a meteor. The meteor site in Mexico is known as the Chicxulub crater.

Dust and particles would have covered Earth for up to ten years.

# After the dinosaurs

## ... in 30 seconds

Dinosaurs may have been wiped out, but some other creatures survived. Following the mass extinction of the dinosaurs, the continents slowly drifted into the positions they are in today, temperatures cooled, and grasslands began to grow.

Mammals—mostly low-browsing plant-eaters—thrived on this new food source, and many of them formed large herds that migrated over the vast green plains. More plant-eaters meant more meat-eaters to hunt them. Insects, reptiles, and sea life began to grow in number again.

This Cenozoic era, the Age of Mammals, began 66 MYA and continues today. It includes mammals, such as saber-toothed tigers and mammoths, which didn't survive the Ice Ages, as well as humans and apes. Today, humans are the planet's dominant species.

But that's not the end of the story for dinosaurs. Their descendants, birds, are found in every part of the world, including Antarctica. There is no doubt that birds today rule the skies now just as their nonavian ancestors once dominated the land. In fact, some baby birds look almost exactly like dinosaurs.

## 3-second sum-up

After the dinosaurs became extinct, other animals became plentiful on land.

## 3-minute mission Endangered ... or extinct?

Dinosaurs are the most famous example of mass extinction, but there have been many more extinctions since the Age of Dinosaurs. When an animal is threatened with extinction, it is known as being critically endangered. There are more than 200 critically endangered mammals in the world right now. Look online or do some research in the library to see which ones are endangered. Find some of the answers on page 96.

In the Cenozoic era, mammals and birds became the dominant creatures on Earth.

Beginning of the Cenozoic era, 66 MYA

*Teleoceras*—early rhinoceros

*Merychippus*— horselike mammal

*Entelodon*— piglike omnivore

Dinosaur fossils from the Mesozoic era (Age of Dinosaurs) 252–66 MYA

# How do we know about dinosaurs?

It wasn't until the 1800s that dinosaur fossils were recognized to be the remains of a type of prehistoric animal. Before then, the strange bones were thought to belong to dragons or giants! But years of scientific study have helped us to understand plenty about dinosaurs—and there is always more to discover. About 700 dinosaur species have been named so far, and a new one is named nearly every week.

# How do we know about dinosaurs?
# Glossary

**adapt** To become better suited to the environment.

**armor** A hard, protective covering over the body of an animal.

**brood** To sit on eggs to hatch them.

**crest** A showy growth on the head of an animal.

**deposits** Sediment and soil that ends up in lakes, usually from rivers flowing down mountains.

**descendant** A living thing that came from an ancestor before it.

**embedded** When something is fixed firmly or deeply in the ground or another object.

**evolution** The process in which changes to plants and animals happen over time.

**gastrolith** A rock held inside an animal to help it grind its food.

**landslide** A collapse of a mass of dirt or rock from a cliff or mountain.

**mammal** An animal that breathes air, has a backbone, and grows hair. Females make milk for their young.

**maniraptoran** A group of advanced theropods thought to be ancestors of both dinosaurs and birds.

**Middle Ages** The period between 500 and 1500 CE.

**mineral** A substance that makes up Earth's rocks, sands, and soil.

**Morrison Formation** A large area of sedimentary rock found in the western United States, where many dinosaur fossils have been found.

**oxygen** A chemical found in the air, which has no color, taste or smell, and that is needed for life.

**paleontologist** A scientist who studies fossils and the history of life.

**predator** An animal that hunts or kills other animals and eats them.

**preserved** When something is kept from rotting or stays in the same state over a long period of time.

**prey** An animal that is hunted or killed by another animal.

**reconstruct** To make something again after it has been destroyed.

**regulate** To control something.

**sauropod** A group of gigantic plant-eating dinosaurs with long necks and small heads.

**scavenge** To feed on dead or decaying plants or animals.

**sediment** Matter that settles to the bottom of a liquid, like soil in a lake.

**species** A group of animals or plants that are similar and can produce young animals or plants.

**talon** A claw, especially belonging to a bird or dinosaur.

**termite** A soft-bodied insect that makes mounds of earth as a nest.

**theropod** A group of meat-eating dinosaurs that had short arms and ran on two legs.

**Tropics** Area just above and below the equator. The climate is warm or hot, and it is wet all year around.

**wishbone** A forked bone between the neck and breast of a bird.

79

# What are fossils?

## ... in 30 seconds

How do we even know dinosaurs existed, let alone what they looked like? From their fossils, of course!

But what are fossils? And how did they stay intact for at least 66 million years? First of all, fossils—the preserved remains of a plant or animal—are extremely rare compared to how many living things have existed on Earth. Most dead animals would have rotted away, their bones and teeth crumbling into dust over time.

But occasionally this didn't happen, like when a dinosaur was stuck in mud. Its body was covered in sediment and difficult to scavenge. Without oxygen reaching it, the body took a long time to decay. Over thousands of years, minerals entered the teeth, bones, and sometimes other remains, such as skin, and hardened them to rock.

Over time, dinosaur fossils have been pushed up to the surface, washed out by water or revealed by landslides. Paleontologists try to put them together, like a 3-D jigsaw with missing pieces. From fossils, they have been able to reconstruct dinosaur skeletons to explain what each one looked like and even understand how they might have lived and died.

## 3-second sum-up

Scientists study dinosaurs by examining fossilized remains preserved in the earth.

## 3-minute mission Show and tell

Found a fossil from your dig (see page 12)? Let's preserve it!
**You need:** Jar • White glue • Water • Paintbrush • Small display case • Pen • Label
1 In a jar, dilute the glue with 4 parts water to 1 part glue.
2 Carefully brush your fossil with the glue and leave to dry.
3 Once dry, place your preserved fossil in the display case, being sure to label it with the correct species name, the part of the body, and the date and place it was found.

# Paleontologists search for dinosaur fossils so they can preserve and study them.

90 MYA—A pack of young *Sinornithomimus* get stuck in the mud and die.

Present day— the pack's fossils are found.

If the body leaves a strong impression in the mud, fossils can show what the skin was like, or if a dinosaur had feathers.

The site is marked off so that the paleontologists can dig out and prepare the fossils.

Once exposed, fossils are protected with plaster coatings and strips made of a coarse woven material.

# Trace fossils

## ... in 30 seconds

Dinosaurs aren't all bones and teeth: eggs, footprints, and even stomach contents, known as cololites, help us figure out how each animal lived. These other fossils are called trace fossils.

**Cololites, as well as fossilized droppings known as coprolites, show us what dinosaurs ate, whether it was plant seeds, insects, or other dinosaurs. Cololites have even shown that some dinosaurs ate their own young in extreme cases!**

Dinosaur teeth are the most common finds, and tell us if the creature could bite through bone, rip into flesh, or strip leaves from trees. Teeth reveal how dinosaurs ate, swallowing whole chunks of flesh, grinding plant matter, or slicing it up. Sometimes, only trackways, or dinosaur footprints, are found, but even these help scientists determine how fast the dinosaur ran, if it lived in groups, or how heavy it was.

Other remains help paleontologists make groundbreaking discoveries. Fossilized *Maiasaura* nests and eggs showed that their newly hatched young were unable to feed themselves; this meant their parents would have raised them, instead of leaving their babies to fend for themselves, as many other dinosaurs were thought to have done.

## 3-second sum-up

Trace fossils and trackways reveal information about how dinosaurs lived.

## 3-minute mission DIY fossils

If you weren't lucky enough to find a fossil on your earlier dig (see page 12), why not make one?
**You need:** 1 quart milk container, cut in half lengthwise • Scissors • Sand • Plaster of Paris • **An adult helper**
1 With an adult's help, cut, then fill the container with sand. Press your foot down in it so it leaves an impression.
2 Mix some plaster and pour it into the container, being sure to completely cover your footprint.
3 Let it set and then carefully remove the "fossil" of your footprint.

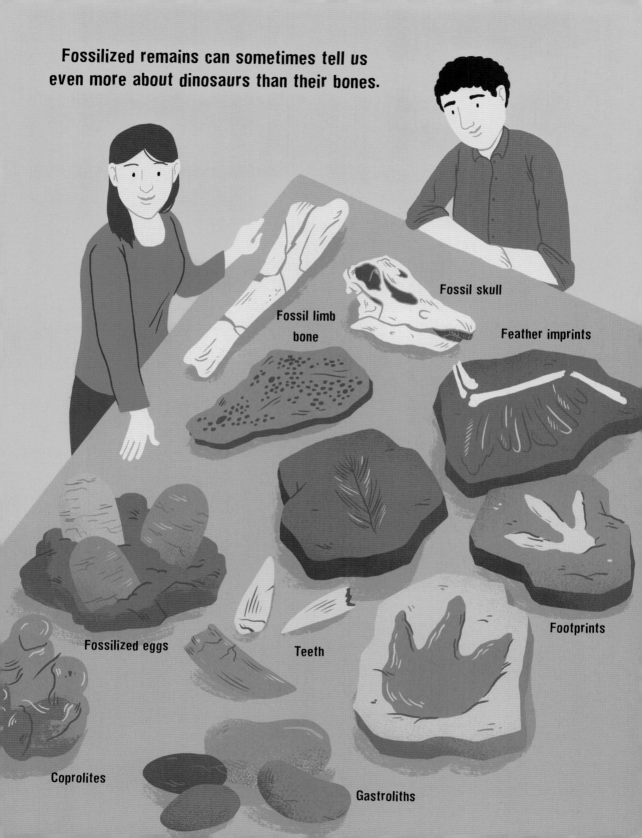

Fossilized remains can sometimes tell us even more about dinosaurs than their bones.

Fossil limb bone

Fossil skull

Feather imprints

Fossilized eggs

Teeth

Footprints

Coprolites

Gastroliths

# Dinosaur detectives

## ... in 30 seconds

Certain fossil finds have led to some of the world's most breathtaking discoveries about dinosaurs. Here are just a few:

There were so many fossils found in the Morrison Formation in the western United States in the late 1800s that it kicked off the "Bone Wars" between two competing paleontologists to see who could identify the most dinosaurs. By the end of it, more than 140 dinosaurs had been identified, including *Stegosaurus, Allosaurus, Diplodocus, Brontosaurus,* and *Brachiosaurus.* In fact, many of the dinosaur bones remain embedded in the rocks for visitors to see.

In the mid-1990s, thousands of remains of "winged" dinosaurs, such as *Confuciusornis* and *Sinosauropteryx,* were found in fine-grain lake deposits in Liaoning, China. Many were even found preserved with downy body feathers. It has since opened up a whole new understanding of feathered dinosaurs and the evolution of flight and birds.

Mongolia's Gobi Desert holds many dinosaur discoveries. Paleontologists have found the preserved skeleton of a mother *Oviraptor* still sitting on her eggs. Even the fossils of a *Velociraptor* and *Protoceratops* were found there, locked in battle. A sandstorm had killed them all immediately.

## 3-second sum-up

Some fossil finds have led to an entirely new understanding of how dinosaurs looked or acted.

### The biggest dinosaur fossil finds

Thigh bone—8 ft (2.4 m) long, *Titanosaur* (1987).
Skull—nearly 10 ft (3 m) long, *Triceratops* (2012).
Longest complete dinosaur skeleton—89 ft (27 m), *Diplodocus* (1901).
Tooth—12 in (30 cm) long, including the root , *T. rex* (1990).

# Some fossil discoveries have led to great breakthroughs in how we understand dinosaurs.

## Bone Wars

In the late 1800s in the United States, Edward Drinker Cope and Othniel Charles Marsh battled to see who could find the most dinosaur fossils in one area.

In over 20 years, they found some of the world's most famous dinosaur fossils.

*Microraptor* fossils were found to have four limbs with feathers, suitable for gliding.

## The link to birds

In the 1990s, fossils and impressions showed evidence of dinosaurs with feathers.

## Building a picture in the sand

The position in which this *Velociraptor* and *Protoceratops* were found indicates that they were fighting. They were found buried in sand and were killed by a sandstorm.

# Miniature dinosaurs?

## ... in 30 seconds

Where do birds come from? Although scientists are still not entirely sure how it happened, they now agree that birds are the direct relatives of dinosaurs.

**Paleontologists are still working on the complex links between dinosaurs and early birds, and they are investigating the evolution of flight and feathers. We now know that some dinosaurs had feathers and even glided from trees with long, feathered limbs. Many theropods known as maniraptorans also had flexible wrists that could have made flight easier.**

Birds and some dinosaurs share many other features, such as brooding on eggs, using brightly colored feathers to attract a mate, and having talons to kill and grasp prey. Birds also share something else in common with dinosaurs—the wishbone.

We may not know the details of how dinosaurs and birds evolved, but one thing is certain: dinosaurs are still alive today. We see them in our yards and towns, in the desert, the Tropics, even Antarctica. In fact, they remain some of the most successful groups of animals ever to exist.

## 3-second sum-up

Scientists now know that birds are the direct descendants of dinosaurs.

## Chickenosaurus?

Hard to believe, but the fantasy of *Jurassic Park*, the 1993 movie where dinosaurs are "grown" again on a tropical island, may actually be possible. After all, scientists have already created ... "Dino-chicken!" By reversing a gene while a baby chicken was still inside its egg, scientists stopped its beak from growing, leaving it with a dinosaur-like "snout." The next step is apparently to give a chicken a tail.

# Birds and dinosaurs share many features.

Birds and dinosaurs are the only animals with wishbones.

Birds may have "shrunk" over time to help them survive, and even switched off a gene to have a beak rather than a jaw with teeth!

Like many birds, dinosaurs are thought to have used brightly colored feathers to attract mates.

Many birds have legs, feet, and claws much like dinosaurs.

**Bird chick**

**Dinosaur chick**

## Evolution of a feather

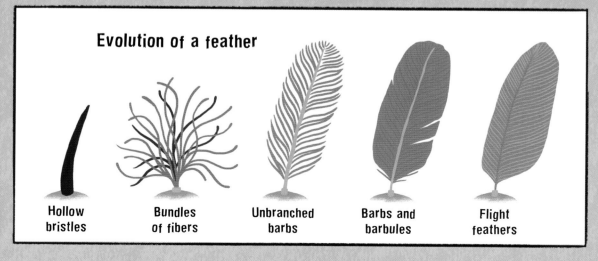

| Hollow bristles | Bundles of fibers | Unbranched barbs | Barbs and barbules | Flight feathers |

# Dinosaur skeletons

## ... in 30 seconds

It is very rare to find a complete dinosaur skeleton. In fact, the chances of any fossilized dinosaur bones surviving in the ground are very low. It was at least 66 million years ago, after all! Yet it is these complete, or articulated, skeletons that reveal the most about how dinosaurs looked and lived.

**But what made them look as they did? Some became huge to defend against other large predators. Others were small to run and hide or get at food that bigger animals would miss. Long legs could run fast; thick legs held more body weight.**

The types of food available also mattered—some dinosaurs evolved strong jaws for crushing plants or cheek pouches for holding plants. Some developed long claws to kill prey or scoop out termite nests and rake leaves off trees. Others began to use their limbs as wings to glide from trees and catch insects. Wherever there was food, a dinosaur adapted a way to get to it!

Dinosaurs didn't only adapt to find food, escape predators, or hunt. Neck frills, head armor, crests, and plates also may have attracted a mate, helped species find each other, or even regulated a dinosaur's temperature.

## 3-second sum-up

Dinosaur skeletons, although rare, give us huge insight into the many types of dinosaurs.

## Two big names!

The name of the largest *T. rex* ever found is Sue (after the person who found it). It may have a friendly sounding name, but, at 13 ft (4 m) tall at the hip, 40 ft (12.3 m) long, and weighing more than 7 tons, it remains a terrifying animal. Sue sold for $7.6 million, the most paid for a dinosaur skeleton. And don't forget Sophie—the world's most complete *Stegosaurus* skeleton, with 85 percent of its bones found, is on display at London's Natural History Museum.

# A *Tyrannosaurus rex* skeleton shows important differences compared to other dinosaurs.

T. rex's brain was the size of a human's. *Stegosaurus*'s was the size of a walnut!

A *T. rex* jaw could crush bone. Other dinosaurs' jaws and teeth were adapted to scoop up plants, eat insects, or catch fish.

A sauropod stomach held huge amounts of plants that it slowly digested, but slender *T. rex* had a fast metabolism.

A stiff tail helped *T. rex* balance as it ran, while *Diplodocus*'s long, thin tail "whipped" its attackers!

Many dinosaurs used claws for defense, like *Iguanodon*'s thumb spike. *T. rex*'s claws were so small that scientists are unsure what they were used for.

Long leg bones helped *T. rex* run fast. Sauropods, however, needed thick, straight legs to hold their weight.

# Changing views

## ... in 30 seconds

Dinosaur bones were first thought to belong to dragons or giants. Without any understanding of what a dinosaur was, this might have made sense in the Middle Ages! Of course, today we know so much about dinosaurs we may think there is little left to surprise us. But as we find more dinosaur fossils and use new technology, we add more fascinating details to the story, even changing parts as we go along.

*Tyrannosaurus rex* is usually shown with scaly, lizardlike skin. But we now know that another large tyrannosaur, *Yutyrannus*, had a coat of feathers. Perhaps all young tyrannosaurs had soft, downy skin, like newborn chicks?

Nearly 100 years ago, a fossil dinosaur was found next to a nest of eggs and named *Oviraptor* ("egg thief") because it was thought to be stealing them for food. But later studies showed it had been brooding its own eggs, like birds. This changed how we thought dinosaurs behaved with their young and also made us rethink their link with birds.

There are still many dinosaur mysteries to solve. Did dinosaurs regulate their temperature like mammals or like reptiles? Were they brightly colored? What kind of sounds did they make? Was *T. rex* just a large scavenger?

## 3-second sum-up

Our views on dinosaurs change all the time and there are still many questions.

## All the colors of the rainbow?

Skin color is an ongoing puzzle. Dinosaurs are usually pictured with gray skin, or colors that helped them blend into their environment. But if such features as crests and neck frills were for display, it seems more probably they would have been brightly decorated or have changed color at times. What do you think?

New discoveries and technology allow
us to find out even more about
dinosaurs, but there are still
puzzles to solve.

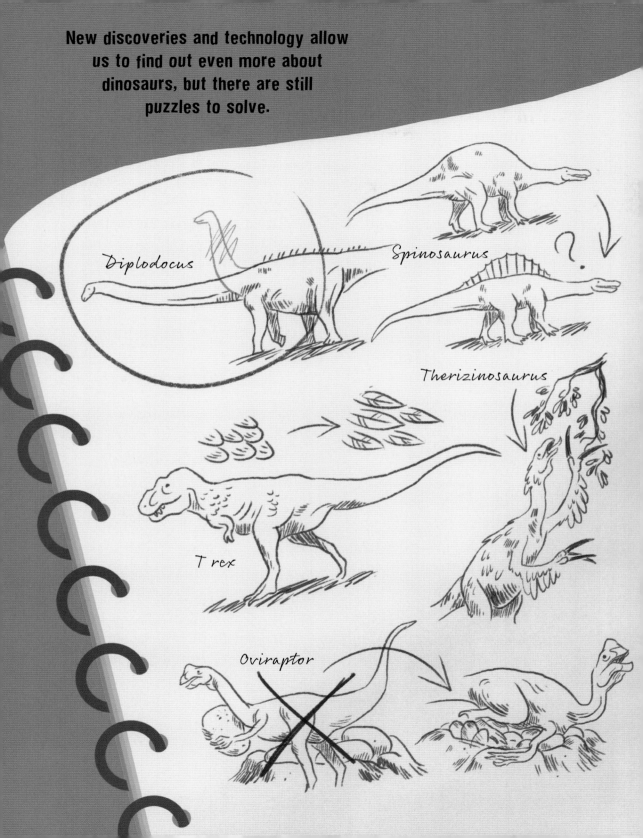

Diplodocus

Spinosaurus

Therizinosaurus

T rex

Oviraptor

# Discover more

## NONFICTION BOOKS

*Dinosaur!*
Dorling Kindersley and Smithsonian
Museum, 2014

*Encyclopedia Prehistoria*
by Robert Sabuda, Matthew
Reinhart
Walker Books Ltd, 2005

*Everything Dinosaurs*
by Blake Hoena
National Geographic Kids, 2014

*Jurassic Survival Guide*
by Heather Dakota
Scholastic, 2015

*Prehistoric Life*
by William Lindsay
DK Publishing, 2012

*The Complete Book of Dinosaurs*
by Dougal Dixon
Southwater, 2012

*The National Geographic Kids
Ultimate Dinopedia:
The Most Complete Dinosaur
Reference Ever*
by Don Lessem
National Geographic Kids, 2010

*The World Encyclopedia of
Dinosaurs & Prehistoric Creatures*
by Dougal Dixon
Southwater, 2014

## DVDS—SUITABLE FOR ALL AGES

**Attenborough and the Giant
Dinosaur**
BBC, 2016

**David Attenborough's Natural
History Museum Alive 3D**
Go Entertain, 2014

**Dinosaurs**
Discovery Channel, 2009

**March of the Dinosaurs**
BBC, 2011

**Planet Dinosaur**
BBC, 2011

**The Four-Winged Dinosaur**
Nova, 2008

**Walking with Dinosaurs**
BBC, 1999

## WEBSITES

**Discovery Kids**
http://discoverykids.com/
category/dinosaurs/

**Miller Museum of Geology, Queen's
University, Ontario, Canada**
http://geol.queensu.ca/museum/
index.php?option=com_content&vi
ew=article&id=78&Itemid=2

National Geographic interactive—take a closer look at bizarre dinosaurs
http://ngm.nationalgeographic.com/2007/12/bizarre-dinosaurs/updike-text.html

**Natural History Museum**
http://www.nhm.ac.uk/discover/dino-directory/index.html

**Smithsonian Museum**
http://paleobiology.si.edu/dinosaurs/

**Sue at the Field Museum**
http://archive.fieldmuseum.org/sue/

*Although every endeavor has been made by the publisher to ensure that all content from these websites is educational material of the highest quality and is age-appropriate, we strongly advise that Internet access is supervised by a responsible adult.*

# Index

# Quiz answers

**Page 14: Convergent evolution**
Spiky plants and animals include cactus, blowfish, porcupine.

**Page 64: Bigger or smaller?**
African elephant: Lighter (6.6 tons)
Blue whale: Heavier (198 tons)
Brown bear: Lighter (0.33 tons)
Saltwater crocodile: Lighter (0.55 tons)

**Page 74: Endangered ... or extinct**
Endangered animals include white rhino, Sumatran tiger, vaquita, western lowland gorilla, Amur leopard, Javan rhino, Sumatran elephant, South China tiger, and Cross River gorilla. For further information, visit www.worldwildlife.org and www.iucn.org.